CCSS **Genre** Fantasy

MW00379865

Essential Question
What insects do you know about?
How are they alike and different?

Come One, Come All

by Sarah Hughes

illustrated by Jason B. Parker

Chapter 1
Planning

Queen Ant was planning a big party. She wanted to invite all of the bugs in the woods.

"What do I need to say?" Queen Ant asked herself.

Come One, Come All
Come to Queen Ant's

Spring Party!

Where:
Queen Ant's Hill

When:
Friday at 2:00

Please bring
something to share.

We will play games.
Please do not
bite or sting.

Queen Ant marched into the woods.

"Please come to my party. We will have a good time!" Queen Ant said to Ladybug, Cricket, and Bee.

"Thank you," Ladybug said with a smile. "I will share some beautiful flowers."

"I will share some honey. And I will leave my stinger at home," Bee said with a laugh.

"I don't know what to share,"
Cricket said with a sigh.

"You can share a song," said Queen
Ant. "We will all listen."

"All right," Cricked replied. "I will
play a song with my wings."

Chapter 2
Getting Ready

Queen Ant baked a pie. Then she looked at the clock. It was late!

"My party starts soon," said Queen Ant. "I have so much to do. I still need to make a banner. How will I finish in time?"

She called Ladybug.

"Hi, Ladybug," said Queen Ant. "Will you please help me? Bring Bee and Cricket, too."

Ladybug, Cricket, and Bee came over.

"Thank you for coming," said Queen Ant. "There is a lot to do."

They all worked together to set up the party.

8

"We are done!" cried Queen Ant. "Thank you, all of you. You were a big help."

"We like to help," said Ladybug.

"Mmm, the pie smells good," said Bee.

"The banner is fancy," Cricket added.

Chapter 3
The Party

All the bugs came to the party. Some jumped, some walked, and some flew.

Bee and Ladybug played a game. Bee threw a ball, and Ladybug caught it.

"Thank you for coming to my party," Queen Ant said to the bugs. "Thank you for bringing something to share. Now Cricket will share a song!"

Cricket rubbed his wings together to play a beautiful tune. When he was done, the bugs clapped. They all had a good time.

Respond to Reading

Retell

Use your own words to retell *Come One, Come All.*

Character	Clue	Point of View

Text Evidence

1. Look at page 4. How does Ladybug feel about the party? What does she say? Point of View

2. Look at page 9. How does Queen Ant feel about her friends?
   Point of View

3. How do you know that *Come One, Come All* is a fantasy? Genre

CCSS Genre Nonfiction

Compare Texts
Compare insect features.

Compare Insects

Digital Vision/Getty Images

Ladybug Parts

wing

head

eye

antenna

legs

Ants and ladybugs are insects. They are alike in many ways. They each have a head, eyes, and six legs. Look at the pictures. Compare a ladybug and a queen ant.

Queen Ant Parts

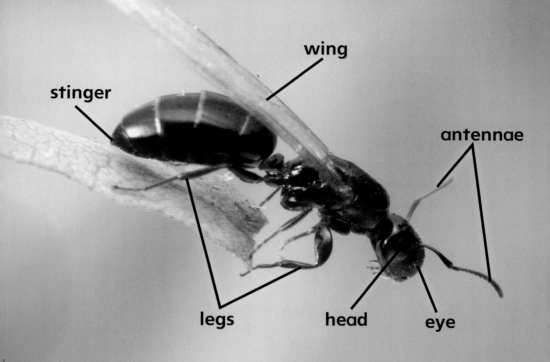

wing

stinger

antennae

legs   head   eye

Nature's Images/Photo Researchers/Getty Images

Make Connections
Look at both selections. Which two insects in *Come One, Come All* have stingers? Text to Text

Focus on
Science

Purpose To compare insects

What to Do

Step 1 ▶ Draw a chart like this one.

Insect	Wings or No Wings

Step 2 ▶ Write the names of the characters in *Come One, Come All* in the chart.

Step 3 ▶ Write *wings* if the insect has wings. Write *no wings* if the insect has no wings.

Conclusion Which insects have wings? Which insects have no wings?